HOW
TO EAT
YOUR
CHRISTMAS
TREE

HOW
TO EAT
YOUR
CHRISTMAS
TREE

Delicious, innovative recipes
for cooking with trees

JULIA
GEORGALLIS

Hardie Grant

BOOKS

Contents

'Use it up,
Wear it out,
Make it do,
Or do without!'

American Office of War, 1944

Introduction

There is a house down the street from me, in a high-up corner of North London where I am from. It looks like it is sinking into the ground, but in reality it is just that the plants in the front garden are growing taller and taller with every month that they are ignored. It is assumed that nobody lives there; the odd one out on a road full of nicely manicured gardens owned by nicely manicured housewives. But then, all of a sudden, incongruous with the rust and mustard palette of the house, stands the most magnificent, bright pastel-blue tree – a blue spruce – nine feet tall and the most alive thing in the garden. A few years ago, on a particularly bitter November evening, with the light fading far too early, I sat in my van opposite the abandoned house with my friend and designer, Lauren Davies. We were staking out the spruce, behaving like a couple of cat burglars: me wearing an incriminating red hat and Lauren, very pregnant, in a badly judged furry leopard-print jacket. When we were sure the coast was clear, I walked up the garden path and rapped on the door handle a few times. Nobody answered. I took out a pair of pliers (because we didn't have any secateurs) and snipped the spiky branches from the tree, being careful not to take any cuttings from under dog-wee height! We were going to take the branches home and eat them.

In the weeks that preceded this shrub-napping, Lauren and I had driven around London and its leafy periphery, trying to procure other types of tree to eat on our ridiculous mission to find some edible conifers. The most successful haul happened at a Christmas tree farm in Kent, where the farmer was so surprised by our request that he gave us Douglas fir and Norway spruce branches at no cost. 'Just make sure you send me some recipes,' he said to us.

'How to eat your Christmas tree...' as Lauren and I called our tree-eating supper club, began in winter 2015, before the noise surrounding issues of waste, reuse, recycling and air quality had been turned up to the max; before the 2018 Intergovernmental Panel on Climate Change published a report[1] giving humans approximately 12 years to keep climate change under control[2]; before British politicians passed a parliamentary motion declaring climate change 'an emergency'.[3] And trees, it would seem, are an integral part of our armoury to stop our carbon emissions rising, acting as sort of 'carbon dioxide vacuum cleaners'.[4] In 2017, Mayor of London, Sadiq Khan, pushed for a huge tree-planting project[5] after the capital's poor air quality was revealed. More recently, there has been international outcry after the dramatic increase of forest fires across the Brazilian Amazon,[6] perhaps linked to new, more intensive deforestation policies[7] introduced by President Jair Bolsonaro. Without enough trees, many believe that future climate control may be impossible.[8] With

this all humming away in the background, each year our supper club has gained more and more traction as people understand the importance of taking care of our environment and limiting waste – especially around the most wasteful (albeit one of the most wonderful) times of year. Even as I write this, I can see the twigs of a bare brown Christmas tree sticking out of the bin next to the pub across the road.

Cue the post-Christmas world. It's nothing like the pre-Christmas world. Everything is glum. We're fatter. We're poorer. We're still a bit hungover. We must repent for all the fun we've had. To top it off, so begins the mass throwing away of millions of little trees – all that was joyful and hopeful about Christmas instead now lines the streets, needle-less, stuffed down the backs of alleyways, damp and sad. I have a sneaking suspicion that this was not how Christmas was supposed to end and an even more sneaking one that perhaps this is not how we were supposed to celebrate Christmas at all.

'Cue the post-Christmas world. It's nothing like the pre-Christmas world. Everything is glum. We're fatter. We're poorer. We're still a bit hungover. We must repent for all the fun we've had. And, to top it off, so begins the mass throwing away of millions of little trees.'

Come December, everything is wrapped in either sugar or bacon and chased with lashings of alcohol, as we are encouraged to consume and gorge our way through this season. I sort of understand this need for abundance, because in one of the most northern parts of the world, we have always felt the need to celebrate something or other around the rubbishest, coldest, darkest, most depressing time of year. It is a time for us to let loose in the bleakest of environments. Pre-Christianity, we Northerners would throw wild parties to try and coax the light back to the world again. Nowadays, we might worship with a mince pie or a turkey or a man climbing down a chimney. But, originally, our ancestors had a party to say thank you to nature. We worshipped the earth, the sun, the water, the sky and the trees, hoping that they would guide us back to the summer. Especially a group of trees that stays leafy all year round, the evergreen, now more commonly known by eye as the Christmas tree.

To us, and to many other cultures around the world, evergreens were revered, seen as sacred symbols of eternity, resilience and strength in the face of adversity, especially in the depths of winter. In Ancient Greece, pine nuts represented eternal life and are still used for burials and funeral rites. Apache Native Americans and Druids both associated pines and firs with the sun. Apaches would include pine nuts in their sunrise ceremonies and Druids would burn firs in the mid-winter in order to encourage the sun to show its face. Eastern Europeans would lay evergreens at the door to keep evil spirits and mud out of the house simultaneously. In China, Korea and Japan the pine, plum and bamboo are known as the 'three friends of winter' – just like the West's Christmas trees, these plants are also resilient to the cold, flourish during wintertime and are often associated with longevity and persistence. Though we associate decorating Christmas trees with a Christian festival, placing trees indoors and decorating them actually has its roots thousands of years before J.C. even had a look in. Egyptians, Greeks, Saxons, Vikings and Romans would also cover their houses with olive, fir, spruce and pine as a part of winter rites.

So... Christmas trees. They're a pretty big deal. We've loved them for a long-time. Except, nowadays, there isn't really so much love for them. They have become commodities of Christmas, treated as nothing more than an expendable crop, appreciated for just a few short weeks and promptly forgotten about for the rest of the year. Trying to eat your tree is not only a way of extending the already-short shelf life of something that has become so inappropriately disposable, but is also an opportunity to really scrutinise keeping Christmas trees in the first place.

I'll be honest with you, it took some work to make something delicious from evergreens. Lauren and I blitzed, blended, smashed and fried. We put some pine needles in a tea strainer and it tasted like wee. We made a weird grass-flavoured scotch egg that made us feel really ill. We deep fried breaded fir needles with disastrous consequences. But we got there in the end: curing, smoking, infusing, baking and pickling our way to a handful of delicious recipes using nuts, berries and needles. Inspiration for this collection of dishes spans as far as the evergreen grows – from Scandinavia, to the Balkans, Southern Europe, the Middle East and Asia. As a baker and chef, the most important thing for me isn't to produce food as a Christmas gimmick or part of the climate change agenda – this recipe book is for taste's sake. Furthermore, it made no sense to produce a set of recipes that bordered on astrophysics, impossible for the home cook to recreate with their own wilting tree. All the recipes included in this cookbook are intended to be not only delectable but very doable at home.

I'm under no illusion that cooking with conifers is going to freeze any ice caps or save any turtles. But our stomach, after all, is our second brain,[9] and food very often makes us think about things that we wouldn't usually think about. As zero-waste chef Anne Marie Bonneau writes, 'We don't need a handful of people being perfectly sustainable – we need millions of people doing it imperfectly.'[10] This is what eating your Christmas tree is all about

– if you think something might be able to be saved or reused, give it a try! In the infographics on pages 24–25, I also highlight what might happen if we stopped cutting down Christmas trees altogether – are there other ways in which we could celebrate Christmas? Could we adorn our houseplants instead (ever heard of the Christmas cactus)? Is there a future where we use bamboo, a much faster growing and more sustainable plant, as a Christmas tree alternative? I really would encourage you, before you throw things away (and I'm not just talking about Christmas trees now) to be both curious and adventurous. Can you replant things? Use it on your skin, clean your house with it or put it in the bath? Eat it rather than bin it? I'm definitely not trying to take the joy out of Christmas or suggest that we spend our entire lives trying to use up every last drop of everything, but it might do our environment (and our pockets!) a favour to think back as to why that object was there in the first place and how throwing it away could be done in a far more sustainable and fun way.

All that is left to say is that I hope you enjoy this set of recipes as much as I have enjoyed serving them up over the last few winters.

Happy experimenting,

JULIA GEORGALLIS

Before You Start

About the recipes

During the course of this book, I have included recipes for cooking with fir, spruce and pine. These three plants taste different, but are interchangeable in each of the recipes that includes them. Using blue spruce or white fir for the Apple & Christmas Tree Membrillo (page 50), for example, would make for two very different outcomes. Fir, spruce and pine are by far the most commonly bought and reliably edible trees. You can eat their needles and use their bark in cooking, though neither of these is particularly pleasant (though not poisonous) if eaten raw. In the Types Of Tree section (pages 29–39), I have included other plants that are arguably more sustainable (the juniper and the bamboo grow far quicker than a conifer ever would and require less energy to plant) and hold similar cultural significance to Christmas trees. I have also included, where necessary, a list of specialist equipment that may be required for some of the recipes.

How do I find a good tree to eat?

A Christmas tree is a crop, just like an apple or an orange. Whether you're going to ingest it or not, it is good practice to make sure that it has been grown with as few chemicals as possible, in a fair environment and either locally and/or sustainably. There have been recent reports that Christmas tree growers and agricultural workers in some parts of the world like Georgia[1] endure poor and dangerous harvesting conditions, and I have come across many trees in the last few years that have been sprayed with chemicals and sometimes paint or glitter, which are bad for the environment and should absolutely not be eaten. It is relatively easy to source responsibly grown Christmas trees online – see page 126 for a list of reputable growers' associations that I have come across, although I am sure there are plenty more. You could also try searching for Christmas tree rentals, which can be returned and replanted once Christmas is over. If possible, buy a live tree and replant it after Christmas to be reused the following year (that is, if you haven't eaten all the needles first and you have somewhere to plant it).

How to prepare your tree needles

Spruce, fir and pine needles can be very sharp, so care must be taken not to hurt your fingers while preparing them for cooking. You will need a pair of large, sharp scissors and a big bowl. Snip some larger branches from your tree. Wash the branches under cold, running water, making sure that you get rid of all possible bits of mud and dirt. You may notice that there are balls of sap, but this is safe to eat, as are the dried buds which might be at the end of some of the branches. Turn the branch upside down over a bowl so that the needles make a chevron shape. Using scissors, cut upwards so that the needles fall directly into the bowl. I usually then wash the snipped needles once more before using them.

Is this going to kill me?

If you stick to pine, fir and spruce, no. However, other common types of trees bought for Christmas include cedar and cypress – both of which are inedible. Yew trees can often be mistaken for Christmas trees but they are INCREDIBLY POISONOUS so don't eat them! Like with any sort of foraging, please make sure you know exactly which plant you are eating before you try it! It should also be noted that all Christmas tree needles are sharp and so you should avoid eating uncooked, un-chopped needles – they're a bit like fishbones and can be just as dangerous. I would also like to point out that any essential oils made from fir, spruce and pine are not really recommended for consumption – just use them for smelling or having a nice massage with.

Sterilising your jars

Quite a few recipes call for sterilisation of glass jars, such as Kilner or Mason jars. There are two ways you can do this. The first is either to wash whichever (preferably recycled) jar you plan on using with hot, soapy water and to stick it in a hot oven set to 100°C (210°F/gas ½) for at least 20 minutes. Alternatively, run your jars through a hot dishwasher cycle. Easy peasy. This will stop your ferments and preserves from going mouldy.

A Note About Plant-Based Diets

This recipe book is about reuse, recycling and resourcefulness – three important elements of sustainability. There are many other ways to embark on an eco-friendlier lifestyle, such as flying less, opting for public transport, avoiding fast fashion, using natural household and personal hygiene products and paying close attention to the way that we eat. Consuming animal products is more detrimental to the planet overall than Christmas tree farming. Animal agriculture takes up more space, more energy and emits gases that contribute to climate change, such as methane. With this in mind, you may question why this book isn't plant-based. These non-veggie recipes come from the earlier, more carnivorous days of the *How To Eat Your Christmas Tree* project and I have left them in, with notes in some cases on vegan/veggie alternatives, for the very fact that they are incredibly tasty. I do strongly suggest, however, treating these recipes (and the choice of consuming animal products in general) carefully.

In the same way that I have talked about treating, sourcing and buying Christmas trees, I would ask that we are all more mindful with our meat, fish and dairy intake. Buy the best quality of these that you can afford, which might mean buying less, but this too is a positive step for the environment. Choosing products that are organic, seasonal and local from small-batch farmers and fishermen who understand how to be sympathetic to the environment is now necessary in a world that is in the midst of a food and agricultural identity crisis. By all means, enjoy your food! But we would also all do well to treat everything that we grow, that is alive in some way, as something that is not expendable and understand that all these things come with a higher environmental price than we might have realised in the past.

How To Have A More Sustainable Christmas

Get rid of the wrap

Don't use wrapping paper, make sure you recycle your cards or, better still, send an e-card! Get in contact with your local council to ask for a more coherent, sustainable and efficient post-Christmas recycling scheme, which includes more visibility on how to recycle Christmas trees, paper, food and, often forgotten, batteries (of which we use A LOT of over the Christmas period).

Do we need to be keeping trees at all?

I know it sounds counterintuitive, as I've just written a book about eating trees, but perhaps the answer is to find another way to celebrate Christmas. Could you draw a tree on some chalkboard or a large sheet of paper, or make a tree out of recycled bits and bobs? Instead of chopping down and buying trees, could you get in touch with your local Christmas tree farmer and ask them to keep the tree planted? Perhaps you could sponsor a tree or find a really great tree planting campaign and support it either financially or by physically spending a weekend outdoors planting in your area. It sounds like a lot more effort than just picking a tree from your local homewares store, but it really does have a positive impact on the environment.

Have yourself a veggie little Christmas

Christmas is definitely a scary time if you're a farm animal. In 2016, it was estimated that 10 million turkeys were eaten on Christmas Day in the UK. But now veggie Christmases in the UK are on the up, rising by 25 per cent in 2019. If you can't do without meat on Christmas Day, no problem, but why not make sure it is a sustainably farmed animal and balance your meat feast by reducing the amount of animal products you eat overall throughout the festive period, and indeed during the rest of the year.

Less stuff, more support

Instead of stocking fillers, concentrate on buying your loved ones environmentally friendly, sustainable and/or charitable gifts. Or, forgo physical gifts altogether and donate to charity or buy/request an experience that you can all do together. Deliveries and internet shopping contribute massively to carbon emissions – try buying your presents from a local producer or shop in person.

New Year's resolutions

Once we're done overdosing on everything over Christmas, it's time to give something up for the beginning of the year. However, instead of imposing impossible promises on yourself, why not make a pledge to the environment? Swap to a plastic-free household, give up as much air travel as possible, try eating meat or fish just once a week... it may be a better way of redirecting your energy.

How To Reuse
Your Christmas Tree

Rather than sneakily leaving your Christmas tree outside the house and praying that someone comes to collect it before June, why not actively dispose of it in a more responsible way that might give it a second life?

Five ways to recycle a tree

1. Recycle it by actively contacting your local council to check with them how you can best recycle your tree.
2. You could also contact your nearest Christmas tree farm to see if they collect and recycle. The farm that supplies me with edible trees turns unsold trees to mulch to use as fertiliser and also makes horse jumps (yup, you read that right) for a neighbouring stable from old Christmas trees.
3. Donate it to a local zoo, safari park or farm for the animals to eat and play with.
4. Buy a real, potted tree and replant it in the garden. I live in an apartment, so my mother's garden has been on the receiving end of all my leftover Christmas trees over the years! If you don't have a space in which to plant, why not ask the council if there is any parkland that might benefit from some new trees? Or even ask a neighbour who does have a garden whether they would like your tree.
5. Dry the branches and use them as winter decorations, or for next year's tree/Christmas wreath! If you really don't have the time or inclination to do this, approach a florist and see if they'd like to have the tree so that they can do something nice with it.

How to replant a Christmas tree

1. You can only repot Christmas trees that still have their root system in place – a cut tree will not regrow.
2. Before planting, make sure your tree gets accustomed to being outdoors again after having being kept nice and toasty for a month. To do this, place it in a cold-ish part of your home; for example, near a drafty door or in a garage. But make sure it still gets plenty of love and some sunlight – don't just stick it in a dark, lonely corridor. Water it once a week. If you live in a particularly cold part of the world where winter may last until March, leave it indoors until spring has well and truly arrived. If the weather is milder, take it outside around the end of January.
3. When you're ready to plant, pick a good spot for your tree. This should be somewhere that isn't too close to the house or other large trees so that it gets enough sunlight and space.
4. Dig a hole that is as deep as the root ball and two to three times wider.
5. Because trees generally go into a sort of hibernation mode in the winter, once it is planted, you don't have to worry about watering it too often. When the weather gets warmer, add more compost and begin to water more.
6. Once your tree is settled in its new earthy home, why not decorate it outside rather than inside each year? It will encourage you to get out into the garden more, even in the cold weather. For a more sustainable angle, ditch the plastic and glass decorations and hang something that the birds might like to eat (page 23).

On Christmas Tree Buds

I'd like to briefly mention Christmas tree buds, which get a bit more attention in the essay 'Scandinavian Taste Buds' (pages 121–123). If you are opting to grow your own Christmas tree, you are in for a real treat in spring when zesty, green buds start to sprout. You can pluck them off the tree, wash them and have a taste! Try adding them to salads, or swapping the needles in the Christmas Tree & Ginger Ice Cream recipe (page 86) and use these instead – they are so delicious!

Seed Baubles

Rather than using not eco-friendly tinsel, energy-leaching lights and unrecyclable plastic to decorate your trees, why not make some biodegradable, potentially EDIBLE decorations? This recipe works really well for birds... and I suppose they could also be eaten by humans, too!

MAKES Enough to decorate a 1.5-metre (5-feet) Christmas tree

PREPARATION TIME 30 minutes to make, then drying overnight

EQUIPMENT some colourful string/yarn and a toothpick

INGREDIENTS 60 ml (2 fl oz/¼ cup) water
3 tbsp agave syrup
2 tsp xanthan gum or vegetarian gel powder
60 g (2 oz/½ cup) flour (rye, wholemeal, spelt and corn work well)
50 g (2 oz/⅓ cup) dried fruit of choice
100 g (3½ oz/¾ cup) seeds (I use a mix of pumpkin, sesame, sunflower and flaxseeds)

METHOD Bring the water and agave syrup to the boil.

Take off the heat and add the xanthan gum, stirring until fully dissolved. Pour the boiling liquid over the flour and mix until combined.

Mix in dried fruit and seeds to the flour mixture – the mixture should be sticky, not watery.

Set the oven to 100°C (210°F/gas ½) and prepare a baking tray (sheet pan) by sprinkling it with flour to stop the ornaments from sticking to the bottom of the tray.

Shape the ornaments while the oven heats up – you can make any shape you like, using cookie cutters or by rolling the seeds into little balls. Remember to add a small hole into the top of each shape using a toothpick and arrange onto the baking tray.

Bake for 1 hour, then leave to dry further, preferably overnight. Once dried, add string to the ornaments and tie to the plants outside!

If We Stopped Harvesting Christmas Trees

See notes on page 129 for processing statistics.

There are an estimated **3 trillion** trees in the world.

170 billion trees are
at risk of destruction.

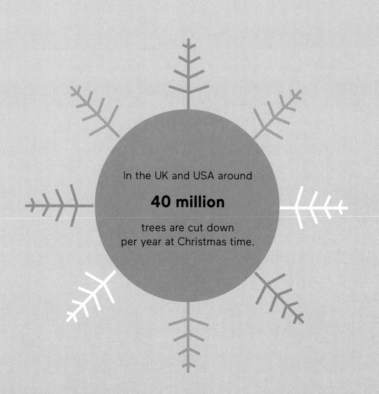

In the UK and USA around

40 million

trees are cut down
per year at Christmas time.

The average Christmas tree is cut down after **7–10 years** of growth.

but the average lifespan of a tree is **400 years old**.

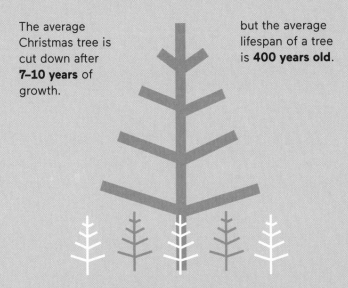

If we let just one year's worth of Christmas trees grow, rather than cut them down, they could absorb over

880,000,000 tonnes

of carbon emissions from the atmosphere throughout their lives, which would be beneficial to the environment.

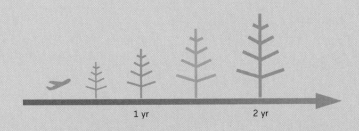

1 yr   2 yr

That's about the equivalent of banning all global air trafiic for just over a year, or taking all cars in the United Kingdom off the road for the next five years...

Types Of Trees

Flavour Profiles & Alternative Christmas Tree Options

Here is a list of trees used over the course of this cookbook. You might be surprised by some of them ...

Bamboo

Family: Poaceae
Use: Shoots and trunk can be eaten; the trunk is also used as a material.

A weird one to start with in a book about cooking with Christmas trees, but bear with me... bamboo is actually one third of the 'three friends of winter' – plum, pine and bamboo. This trio represents, culturally, a similar group of trees to conifers in Chinese, Korean and Japanese folklore. Bamboo is a symbol of resilience and abundant growth. As a versatile, evergreen grass, it probably deserves a whole book to itself as its uses are so widespread, from eating it to building with it. If we were to use bamboo as a Christmas tree instead of spruce or pine, we might be better off as it is one of the fastest growing plants on earth and requires a lot less energy to grow.

caution

Cypress & Cedar

These trees are often sold as Christmas trees. Neither one of them is edible and must NOT be used for consumption.

Juniper

Family: Cypress
Use: The berries are widely used in cooking and as part of the gin-making process

Junipers have a lot to say for themselves. They grow everywhere, from the Arctic to Africa. While they aren't usually used as Christmas trees, probably because they grow in irregular shapes, they look an awful lot like Christmas trees and hold the same symbolism for being hardy, plucky plants with spirit in the face of hardship. Their small, spiky needles don't give a very strong flavour, but the purple berries are used widely in cooking and herbal remedies. They are one of the key components of gin and have a peppery, floral taste. I have used them a lot in this cookbook, which you might think is cheating, but their flavour is immensely adaptable and works well with everything from salty, meaty dishes to sharp, fruity flavours. In folklore, it seems like juniper berries have been used for everything, from curing tapeworms to sprucing up love potions.

Fir

Family: Pinaceae
Types of tree: Noble fir, Balsam fir, Douglas fir, Nordmann fir, Canaan fir, Fraser fir, white fir, grand fir or Korean fir
Use: Needles used for infusions

Fir trees are the more usual, most popular Christmas tree choice in the UK. They have large, feathery needles that don't dry out or drop quickly. With a zesty, grassy taste, fir pairs well with citrussy, sharp flavours and is commonly used in alcoholic drinks. A very well-travelled plant, they grow in the Americas, Europe, North Africa and Asia. The Celts believed that firs were one of the nine sacred trees and they were used in important ceremonies.

Olives

Family: Oleaceae
Use: Leaves are used for ceremonies and eating, oil and fruit are used in cooking

In my opinion, the olive is the OG Christmas tree. Olives are found in warmer climates like Southern Europe and the Middle East and were thought of as symbols of eternal life. They may not be a conifer and don't look as good covered in baubles and Christmas lights, but they are evergreens nonetheless and are used culturally in a very similar way – to symbolise steadfastness and resilience in harsh (in this case, hot and dry) environments. Olive oil is a key component of many European, Middle Eastern and Central Asian cuisines – it is the elixir of life, well known for its youth-giving properties. It has a smoky, warm flavour with lots of mouthfeel. Olive leaves are lesser used, but can be brewed to make tea or used as a herb – they have a woody flavour. The fruit itself is salty, meaty and comes in many sizes and colours.

Plum

Family: Prunus
Use: Edible fruit

Another funny thing to put in a book about eating Christmas trees but, like bamboo, plums are part of the 'three friends of winter' – plum, pine and bamboo. These represent a similar group of trees to conifers in Chinese, Korean and Japanese folklore. The plum stands for hope and perseverance. They are courageous, bright little plants, and humans have had a long love affair with them – plums were one of the first fruits to be domesticated. They range from sweet to sour and work well in both savoury and sweet dishes.

Pine

Family: Pinaceae
Type of trees: Afghan pine, Austrian pine, red pine, white pine, Scots/Scotch pine, lodgepole pine, ponderosa pine or Virginia pine
Use: Nuts used in cooking, needles used in infusions

Pine trees are found across almost all of the Northern Hemisphere – their scent is the definition of Christmas. The flavour of pine needles is not very strong but pine nuts, which come from the middle of the newly-formed pine cones, are incredibly useful and popular in cooking. They are warm, oily and woody and add a lovely creaminess to any dish. Pines have a very long, rich history in folklore around the world. In Ancient Egypt and Greece, they were used in burials due to their association with eternal life. Pine cones were also used as fertility amulets by Ancient Greeks and Native Americans. In Central Asia, pine forests were seen as sacred; a place for shamanistic healing and reverence. Both Druids and Central American tribes used pine in sacred sun ceremonies.

Spruce

Family: Pinaceae
Type of trees: Norway spruce, blue spruce, white spruce, Black Hills spruce, Colorado spruce or Serbian spruce
Use: Needles used for infusions and for flavour, new buds can be eaten

In my humble opinion, blue spruce is the most delicious of all Christmas trees. Their needles and buds have an incredibly strong floral flavour that borders on vanilla and orange. Norway and Blue spruce are popular choices for Christmas trees but the needles are sharp and drop quickly once cut, so they are the messier option. I recommend buying a living tree and replanting it once Christmas is over so that you can enjoy the spruce buds that arrive in the spring. Spruce trees are found in colder parts of the world – mainly the Northern hemisphere. One of the oldest trees in the world happens to be a spruce – his name is Old Tjikko and he has lived in Sweden for approximately 9,550 years.

Planting Alternative Christmas Trees

Not everyone has a large enough garden space to plant a Christmas tree – many of which end up growing to potentially gigantic proportions. If space is an issue, or you would like to have some fun growing your own plants indoors, try planting one of these alternative Christmas trees...

Bamboo

Where to plant: In soil, either indoors or outdoors or can be kept in a vase of water for up to two years
When to plant: In the spring
Where to buy: Buy rhizomes in reputable plant nurseries

Bamboo is the Asian equivalent of the traditional Christmas tree, representing longevity, resilience and hope in the face of adversity. It grows well in many climates and most species are fully hardy. Rhizomes are the woody, bottom parts of the bamboo – they look lovely when kept in a vase with some water and will continue to grow for two or three years without soil. They can also be planted, preferably in the spring, in soil either inside or outside. Please note that bamboo is a fast growing, invasive plant – stop it from getting out of control by digging a trench, roughly 20 cm (8 in) wide, all the way around the bamboo, or by keeping it potted.

How to plant bamboo rhizome
1. Dig a hole twice the depth of the root ball.
2. Sink the bamboo in the hole and cover the root and the bottom of the rhizome in soil, making sure that it is firmly in the ground.
3. Bamboo tolerates most soil, but does not like being soggy and also can't stand very dry conditions, so make sure you get the balance right. Water more regularly in the spring and summer, as bamboo is dormant from autumn until the beginning of spring.

Juniper

Where to plant: Outdoors
When to plant: All year round
Where to buy: Buy saplings online, The Woodland Trust stocks them

Juniper is a festive, evergreen tree that can be planted all year round. It is fantastic for the garden as birds snack on the berries and it is an easy plant to grow if you are a beginner to gardening. The berries can also be picked, dried and used in some of the recipes for this book. It is tolerant of most soils, but needs to be kept well drained. As your sapling grows, it may need occasional pruning as it can become unruly.

How to plant juniper saplings

1. Dig a hole twice the depth of the sapling's root ball, sink the sapling into the hole and cover with soil.
2. The sapling requires a little more TLC in the first month – water it two to three times a week during this time, then you can leave it to do its thing! It does not like to be too wet.

Olive

Where to plant: Indoors or outdoors
When to plant: All year round, as long as the ground isn't frozen
Where to buy: Buy trees and saplings online

Contrary to popular belief, olive trees CAN grow in colder climates – in fact, they need two or three months of cold weather per year to fruit. They are hardy up until -15°C (5°F). Olives are the OG Christmas trees, used by the Romans and Ancient Greeks to celebrate eternal life and winter rites. Olive trees take years to grow and are happy both indoors and outdoors.

Planting an olive sapling

1. Dig a hole twice the size of the root ball. Sink the tree or sapling into the hole and spread the roots out.
2. Fill the hole with soil and pat down. For the first couple of years you have the option of using a support for your tree to encourage it to grow into a stable trunk.
3. Even though olives are drought resistant and don't require a huge amount of water, make sure that the soil is never totally parched.

Plum

Where to plant: Plant from pit indoors, then move outside when it gets big enough
When to plant: Late winter, early spring
Where to buy: Reuse your plum pits!

Plums are good fun! They are one of the 'three friends of winter' along with the pine and bamboo, and have a reputation for being hopeful, plucky plants, just like the Western Christmas tree! There are many species of plum, which means that certain species could be suitable even for the smallest of gardens. Next time you eat a plum, consider saving the pit – keep them once you have eaten the fruit and grow these into a new plum tree.

Planting a plum from pit

1. Dry the pit on the window sill for 4 days. Once dried, crack open and take out the almond-shaped seed from the middle. Make sure that the seed is viable by placing it in a cup of water. It should sink to the bottom of the cup – if it floats it is not suitable for planting.
2. Fold the viable seeds between a damp, paper towel. Place the towel in an airtight container/bag and leave in the coldest part of your refrigerator for 4 weeks.
3. After a month or so, the seeds should have started to germinate and sprout. If not, keep checking on them until they have started to sprout.
4. After sprouts start forming, prepare a pot full of soil. Push your thumb into the middle of the pot and place the seed in the soil, root down, sprout up. Cover with more soil. It will take a few months for the sprout to push through the surface, so be patient and make sure you keep the plum plant moist in a bright spot but away from direct sunlight.

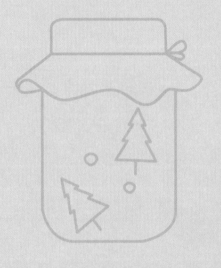

Ferments
&
Preserves

Christmas-Cured Fish

Cured fish is wonderful for starters (appetisers), breakfast, or in a very decadent sandwich. Trout is a great option for curing or use other sustainable fish, such as monkfish, halibut, or something recommended by your local fishmonger. Use the freshest fish you can find, making sure it hasn't been frozen before buying.

MAKES	2 kg (4 lb 8 oz) of fish
PREPARATION TIME	30 minutes + minimum 24 hours, maximum 36 hours curing time

INGREDIENTS

2 kg (4 lb 8 oz) filleted fish of your choice
350 g (12 oz) fir or spruce needles or 700 g (1 lb 9 oz) pine needles (or a combination)

770 g (1 lb 11 oz/ 3⅓ cups) demerara sugar
500 g (1 lb 2 oz/ 1½ cups) table salt
2 small beetroots (beets), grated
grated zest of 3 lemons

METHOD

Before you cure, it is good practice to freeze the fish as this kills any bacteria that might be present. You can 'flash freeze' for 24 hours, but I like to freeze the fish for about a week. Defrost it in the refrigerator a few hours before you start curing.

Prepare the needles (page 15).

To make the cure, mix the sugar, salt, grated beetroot, lemon zest and needles together.

Lay out some cling film (plastic wrap) on a flat surface and sprinkle a generous layer of the curing mixture over it, making sure it is roughly the length and width of the fillet.

You might need an extra pair of hands for this next step: lay the fish over the first layer of cure, then pack the top and sides of the fillet with the rest of the cure and wrap tightly in cling film, making sure it is totally covered in the cure mixture.

Place the fish on a baking tray (sheet pan) underneath something heavy, and refrigerate between 24 and 36 hours. Halfway through the curing process, turn the fish over, remembering to place it under something heavy again.

When it is ready to eat, wash off the cure and make sure there are no needles left on the fish. Slice thinly.

This keeps in the refrigerator for up to 5 days.

Christmas Tree Vinegar

This is by far the easiest way to reuse your Christmas tree – whatever kind of tree you might have. It's quick and a great way of using up particularly dry trees.

MAKES Enough to fill a 2-litre (70-fl oz/8-cup) jar

PREPARATION TIME 30 minutes + up to 3 months (minimum 2 weeks) infusion time

EQUIPMENT 2 x large glass jars with lids, a Kilner or Mason jar is ideal

INGREDIENTS 2 litres (70 fl oz/8 cups) of good-quality cider vinegar

200 g (7 oz) fir, pine or spruce needles (or a combination of these)

METHOD Sterilise the glass jars that you are going to use (page 15).

Prepare and finely chop the needles (page 15).

Pour the vinegar into a large saucepan and heat over a medium heat until warm but not boiling.

Add the chopped needles to the sterilised jar and, using a funnel, pour in the warmed vinegar.

Tightly seal the jar and leave to infuse for at least 2 weeks and up to 3 months. You will know when your vinegar is infused as the needles will start to sink slowly to the bottom of the jar.

Once infused, use a fine sieve (fine mesh strainer) to strain out all of the needles and pour the strained vinegar into a new, sterilised jar. Once infused, the vinegar keeps for years.

Tip: This Christmas tree vinegar is the perfect homemade festive gift.

Christmas Tree
& Beetroot Pickled Eggs

Pickled eggs are vastly under-appreciated, under-eaten and under-represented and I only wish that people would start to enjoy them more. Great for canapés, picnics and showing off in general, especially as the beetroot gives the eggs such a beautiful, vibrant colour!

MAKES 8 pickled eggs

PREPARATION TIME 30 minutes + 1–3 days pickling time

EQUIPMENT a large glass jar with a lid, a Kilner or Mason jar is ideal

INGREDIENTS

a handful of spruce or fir needles (or 2 handfuls if using apple cider vinegar)
8 large organic free-range eggs
600 ml (20 fl oz/ 2½ cups) Christmas Tree Vinegar (page 44) or apple cider vinegar
75 g (2½ oz/¼ cup) sea salt flakes
100 g (3½ oz/½ cup) demerara sugar
1 small beetroot (beet), peeled and roughly chopped

METHOD

Sterilise the jar and prepare the needles (page 15).

Boil the eggs for 7 minutes exactly then immerse quickly in cold water. Once cooled, peel the shells from the eggs.

In a small saucepan, heat up the vinegar, salt and sugar until just boiling.

Arrange the beetroot, needles and eggs in the jar and pour over the hot pickling liquid.

Tightly seal the jar. Once cooled, place the jar in the refrigerator and leave for at least 24 hours (or 36 hours if using apple cider vinegar) before eating. I don't recommend curing for longer than 3 days as the eggs become tough. Once opened they are best eaten within 2 days.

Christmas Tree Pickles

I love a good pickle. Either use infused Christmas Tree Vinegar (page 44) to make these or use fresh needles and leave to pickle for a couple of extra weeks. Use whichever vegetable you like and is in season. Carrots and cucumbers work well and add beetroot (beets) for some extra colour.

MAKES Enough to fill a 2-litre (70-fl oz/8-cup) jar

PREPARATION TIME 3 days + 1 month (minimum 5 days) pickling time

EQUIPMENT a 2-litre (70-fl oz/8-cups) glass jar with a lid, a Kilner or Mason jar is ideal

INGREDIENTS
a handful of spruce, pine or fir needles
2 litres (70 fl oz/8 cups) either Christmas Tree Vinegar (page 44) or apple cider vinegar
50 g (2 oz/½ cup) salt flakes
900 g (2 lb/4 cups) demerara sugar

700 g (1 lb 9 oz) ribbons of beetroot (beets), carrots, cucumber (preferably a mix of all three)
a handful of juniper berries

METHOD Sterilise the jar and prepare the needles (page 15).

In a saucepan, heat up the vinegar, salt and sugar until just boiling.

Arrange the beetroot, carrots, cucumber, needles and juniper berries at the bottom of the jar and pour in the pickling liquid.

Tightly seal the jar. Turn it upside down once, quickly, to get rid of any extra air. Once cooled, either leave in a cool, dark place or in the refrigerator. Leave for a minimum of 5 days before opening. Keep for 2 weeks once opened.

Apple & Christmas Tree Membrillo

Membrillo is a sliceable Spanish-style jam (jelly) and is wonderful when eaten with cheese. This is quite a fiddly but satisfying recipe, usually made from quince, which contains a lot of pectin – the reason why membrillo has such a strong structure. I have swapped the quince for apples, which complements the flavour of Christmas trees. I recommend using just fir or spruce as pine is too delicate a flavour for the zesty apples. The interesting thing about the texture of this membrillo is that even when it has set, it is still soft because of the oils in the Christmas tree needles.

MAKES Enough to fill a 15-cm (6-in) glass oven dish

PREPARATION TIME 2 hours + 10 days–2 weeks setting time

INGREDIENTS 1 kg (2 lb 4 oz) apples (about 10 apples)
100 ml (3½ fl oz/scant ½ cup) water
40 g (1½ oz) fir or spruce needles
caster (superfine) sugar
juice of 2 lemons

METHOD Peel and core the apples and place in a saucepan. Add the water and bring to the boil. Simmer until the apples are very soft, around 30 minutes.

Meanwhile prepare the needles (page 15), then blitz for 3 seconds in a food processor.

Mash or purée the boiled apples, then weigh them.

Weigh out the same amount of sugar to apples (approx. 1 kg/2 lb 4 oz/4⅓ cups) and add this to the pan with the apples. Heat the pan over a medium heat until the sugar has dissolved.

Add the lemon juice and needles to the apple and sugar mix. Bring to the boil for a few seconds, then simmer, stirring continuously for about 30 minutes.

Before the membrillo really starts to set, take the mixture off the heat and strain the needles out using a fine sieve (fine mesh strainer). Put the needle-less membrillo back on the heat and continue to stir for approximately 30 minutes more.

You will know when your membrillo is ready when it begins to turn either dark green or dark red (depending on the type of apples you are using) and/or the mixture has started to come away from the pan and/or when a wooden spoon leaves a definite trace through the mixture.

Prepare a 15-cm (6-in) glass oven dish with some greaseproof paper and pour in the hot mixture. Wrap the dish tightly with a dish towel so that it is airtight and leave to set in a cool, dark place for between 10 days and 2 weeks.

Once it has set, it keeps for about 3 months, provided it is well wrapped. Store at room temperature. Will keep, wrapped, for 3 months. Once unwrapped, keep in the fridge for 5 days

See recipe photo overleaf.

Chicken Liver & Sloe Gin Pâté

The key component of gin is juniper, which I have referred to in this book as a Christmas tree alternative. The sweet and floral flavours of sloe gin work really well with the rich flavour of chicken livers. This recipe won't be as thick as shop-bought pâté because alcohol acts as a thinner, but you can counteract this by using a really thick double (heavy) cream.

MAKES Enough for 4 people as a starter

PREPARATION TIME 25 minutes

INGREDIENTS

250 g (9 oz) unsalted butter
1 red onion, roughly chopped
1 clove garlic, chopped
3 heaped tsp crushed juniper berries
400 g (14 oz) whole chicken livers
150 ml (5 fl oz/scant ⅔ cup) double (heavy) cream
6 tbsp good-quality gin or sloe gin
a handful of thyme leaves
sea salt and freshly ground black pepper

METHOD

Melt 50 g (2 oz) of the butter in a frying pan (skillet) with the onion and garlic for about 5 minutes over a medium heat.

Add 1 heaped teaspoon of the juniper berries and all of the chicken livers. Fry for another 5 minutes, until the livers are browned. Switch-off the heat and allow the livers to cool slightly, then blend in a food processor with the double cream and gin, until smooth.

Melt the remaining butter in the frying pan, with the remaining juniper berries. Add the thyme then season well with salt and pepper.

Place the blended liver mixture in four small ceramic pots and pour over the melted butter.

Chill the pâté in the refrigerator where it will keep for 3 days. It can be kept frozen for 3 months.

Sour Plum Pickle

This recipe is inspired by the flavour of Japanese umeboshi, and is a homage to the plum, which is one third of the Asian 'three friends of winter'. In June, umeboshi is made across Japan by salting ume (Japanese sour plums or apricots). Making umeboshi is a very labour-intensive process and it is hard to find ume outside of Japan. So this recipe is for a very quick sour plum pickle instead, using whichever variety of plum that you can find.

MAKES 1 kg (2 lb 4 oz) of pickle

PREPARATION TIME 20 minutes + 1 month (minimum 2 weeks) pickling time

EQUIPMENT a large glass jar with a lid, a Kilner or Mason jar is ideal

INGREDIENTS

500 ml (34 fl oz/4 cups) rice wine vinegar
25 g (2 oz/½ cup) sea salt flakes
150 g (10½ oz/ 1⅓ cups) demerara sugar
500 g (1 lb 1 oz) plums, halved and depitted

2 bay leaves
½ tsp fennel seeds
½ tsp aniseed
2 cinnamon sticks
½ tsp cloves
1 tsp star anise

METHOD

Sterilise the jar (page 15).

In a saucepan, heat up the rice vinegar, salt and sugar until just boiling.

Arrange the plums, herbs and spices at the bottom of the jar and pour in the pickling liquid.

Tightly seal the jar. Turn upside down once, quickly, to get rid of any extra air. Leave to cool then place in the refrigerator.

Leave for a minimum of 2 weeks before opening. Store unopened in a cool, dark place. It keeps for up to 6 months unopened – the longer the plums are left to pickle, the softer they will become. Once opened, keeps in the refrigerator for a week.

Cherry & Juniper Jam

Though juniper, an evergreen and a cousin of the Christmas tree as we know it, has a lovely, festive flavour, this jam (jelly) is great all year round, especially in the summer when cherries are in season. Perfect either on toast for breakfast or as part of a cheese course.

MAKES Enough to fill a 750 g (1 lb 10 oz) jam jar

PREPARATION TIME 2 hours, 15 minutes

EQUIPMENT sterilised jam (jelly) jars with lids

INGREDIENTS
600 g (1 lb 5 oz) cherries
300 ml (10 fl oz/ 1¼ cups) water
5 tsp crushed juniper berries

450 g (1 lb/2 cups) caster (superfine) sugar
juice of 2 lemons

METHOD Halve and destone the cherries.

Add the cherries, water, juniper berries, sugar and lemon juice to a heavy-bottomed saucepan and bring to the boil.

Once the mixture is boiling, turn down the heat to low-medium and simmer until the cherries have reduced and all the water has gone. This should take about 2 hours.

Alternatively, you can use a sugar thermometer to set your jam. Boil until the mixture reaches 104°C (219°F), then keep it at this temperature for 5 minutes.

Meanwhile, sterilise the jam jars (page 15).

Once the jam is ready, fill the jars to the brim and seal the lid well. Turn upside down once, quickly, to get rid of any excess air. Leave to cool. The jam will keep well, unopened, for up to 6 months. Once opened, keeps in the refrigerator for a week.

Feast
Food

Gin Pulled Lamb
with thyme & alcoholic apricots

An unlikely match, but floral juniper flavours complement sweet apricots really well. It is an easy dish to prepare, you just need to season it well enough and have enough patience to roast the lamb for up to 8 hours until the meat falls off the bone. When buying lamb, make sure that it has been responsibly sourced by talking to your butcher – buy the best quality that you can afford/ available to you. Jackfruit is also a remarkable vegan substitute to lamb, as it 'pulls apart' well.

MAKES Enough for 10 people as a main

PREPARATION TIME 20 minutes, plus overnight infusing, then 7–8 hours cooking

INGREDIENTS

300 g (10½ oz) apricots
a bottle of really nice gin
1.5 kg (3 lb 5 oz) lamb
  shoulder or jackfruit
2 onions
3 garlic cloves
a bunch of thyme sprigs
sea salt and freshly
ground black pepper
500 ml (17 fl oz/2 cups)
  water
150 g (5 oz) unsalted
  butter
lots of olive oil
Retsina Squash (see
  opposite), to serve

METHOD

In a bowl, cover the apricots with 375 ml (12½ fl oz/1½ cups) of the gin and leave to infuse overnight. The next day, preheat the oven to 180°C (350°F/gas 6).

Arrange the lamb on a large baking tray (sheet pan), add the onions, garlic, half the thyme sprigs and season well. Add the water, cover with kitchen foil and roast in the oven for 4 hours until the meat starts to fall off the bone.

Add the butter, a generous glug of gin and the rest of the thyme to the roasted lamb. Turn the oven down to 140°C (275°F/gas ½). Return to the oven for a further 3–4 hours, mixing every hour so that the fat is evenly distributed. Add the marinated apricots about 20 minutes before the meat is ready so that they heat up but don't burn.

When the meat pulls apart easily, add olive oil, a splash more gin and serve with retsina squash.

Retsina Squash
with preserved lemons, sultanas & rosemary

Retsina is a dry wine infused with the sap of Aleppo pine. The Greeks have been infusing wine with pine sap to sweeten it since Ancient times.

MAKES Enough for 4 people as a main

PREPARATION TIME 40 minutes, plus overnight soaking

INGREDIENTS

200 g (7 oz/1²/₃ cups) sultanas (golden raisins)
a bottle of retsina
2 large squash (anything that's in season)
a bunch of rosemary
sea salt and freshly ground black pepper
olive oil, for drizzling
200 g (7 oz/2¼ cups) flaked almonds
200 g (7 oz) preserved lemons
Gin Pulled Lamb (see opposite) or Pine Nut Couscous (page 68), to serve

METHOD Cover the sultanas with 300 ml (10 fl oz/1¼ cups) of the retsina and leave to soak overnight. The next day, preheat the oven to 200°C (400°F/gas 6).

Cut up the squash so each piece is 4 cm (1.5 in) thick, leaving the skin on. Arrange the squash on a baking tray (sheet pan) with the rosemary, season well, and drizzle with olive oil. Bake in the oven, uncovered, for 20 minutes, until soft.

Meanwhile, toast the almonds in a dry frying pan (skillet) so that they are just browned.

Add the marinated sultanas, preserved lemons and toasted almonds to the squash and bake for another 15 minutes.

When cooked, add a splash more retsina and a drizzle of olive oil. Serve warm with gin pulled lamb or pine nut couscous.

See recipe photos on previous page.

Pine Nut Couscous
with pomegranates, oranges & mint

There is nothing sadder than couscous which is sparingly flavoured. The sharpness of pomegranates works well with the creaminess of the pine nuts. This dish is brilliant as an accompaniment to meat and vegetables and works particularly well with the the mushroom, pine nut and sourdough recipe opposite.

MAKES   Enough for 10 people as a side

PREPARATION TIME   15 minutes, plus overnight soaking

INGREDIENTS   seeds from 2 pomegranates
150 g (5 oz/1¼ cups) sultanas (golden raisins)
juice of 2 oranges, zest of 1
500 g (1 lb 2 oz/ 2¾ cups) couscous
a vegetable stock cube
100 ml (3½ fl oz/scant ½ cup) olive oil or vegetable butter
2 bunches of mint, chopped
200 g (7 oz/1⅓ cups) pine nuts

METHOD   Cover the pomegranate seeds and sultanas in the orange juice (and any pomegranate juice you might have been able to save) and leave to soak overnight.

The next day, measure out the couscous into a saucepan and place the stock cube on top.

Cover the couscous with double the volume of boiling water and cover the pan with a lid.

After 15 minutes, the water should have been absorbed into the couscous. If not, stir and leave it for a few more minutes.

Add the olive oil to the couscous and fluff it with a fork, making sure that the stock cube and oil are evenly distributed through the couscous.

Add the chopped mint, soaked fruit and pine nuts. Mix together and serve immediately.

Stuffed Mushrooms
with pine nuts, pistachio & sourdough

As pine nuts are always easy to get hold of, this recipe can be made at any time of year. Plus this is an excellent way of using up leftover bread.

MAKES Enough for 2 people as a main
or 4 people as a side

PREPARATION TIME 35 minutes

INGREDIENTS

120 g (4 oz/¾ cup)
pine nuts
100 g (3½ oz/
1 cup) sourdough
breadcrumbs
200 g (7 oz/1½ cups)
pistachios, crushed
120 ml (4 fl oz/½ cup)
olive oil or vegetable
butter, at room
temperature

2 small garlic cloves,
chopped
800 g (1 lb 12 oz)
mushrooms (anything
stuffable), stalks
removed
sea salt and freshly
ground black pepper

METHOD Lightly toast the pine nuts and breadcrumbs in a dry frying pan (skillet).

Combine the pistachios, pine nuts, breadcrumbs, olive oil or vegetable butter and garlic in a mixing bowl.

Lay out the mushrooms in a baking dish with the underside facing upwards. Stuff the middle of each mushroom with some of the pine nut and breadcrumb mixture, making sure it is evenly distributed between each mushroom. Season with salt and pepper.

Grill (broil) the stuffed mushrooms for 20 minutes until pine nuts brown and breadcrumbs are crispy. Serve immediately.

See recipe photo on previous page.

Christmas Tree Ash

Ash is used in cooking all over the world and is having a bit of a moment as top chefs and restaurants such as NOMA begin to use more of it. A revelation to me was the discovery of Christmas Tree Ash – which is what you get when you incinerate some Christmas trees in an oven. It is easy to make and leaves you with a valuable, aromatic ingredient that can be kept and used on all sorts of things.

MAKES Enough to fill a small plastic container, around 12 x 17 cm (5 x 7 in) in size

PREPARATION TIME 35 minutes

EQUIPMENT a baking tray and a wire cooling rack

INGREDIENTS a large handful of
Christmas tree
branches

METHOD Preheat the oven, turning it up as hot as it will go.

Take the branches of your Christmas tree and wash any dirt from them.

Place the branches on a rack over a baking tray (sheet pan) and bake them until they are completely and utterly burnt.

Turn the oven off and let them cool down.

Blitz the branches in a food processor until they become a fine powder.

Transfer to an airtight container and store in a cool, dark place where the ash will keep for about 6 months.

Burnt Ash Cauliflower

Musky cauliflower is tough enough to carry the aromatic and oily flavours of the pine-ash butter as well as a smoky, crispy chargrilled texture.

MAKES Enough for 4 people as a main

PREPARATION TIME 1 hour

INGREDIENTS

2 large cauliflowers,
   leaves removed
2 tbsp of Christmas
   Tree Ash (page 71)
150 g (5 oz) good-
   quality unsalted butter,
   softened

a pinch of salt and
   freshly ground black
   pepper
Pine Nut Couscous
   (page 68) and tzatziki
   and yoghurt, to serve

METHOD Steam the cauliflowers for 30 minutes until slightly soft.

Meanwhile, add 1 tablespoon of Christmas tree ash to the butter.

Cut the cauliflowers into 2.5 cm- (1 in-) thick slices then melt the butter in a large frying pan (skillet).

Fry the slices of cauliflower in the ash-butter until they are slightly blackened. You may need to use two frying pans to do this or fry them in batches and keep the rest in a warming oven.

Season to taste. Serve with pine nut couscous and a dollop of tzatziki or yoghurt.

Ash Baked Vegetables

You can use whichever vegetable you prefer or is in season, but combining the earthy flavour of the pine-ash with root vegetables makes for a very festive dish indeed.

MAKES	Enough for 4 people as a side
PREPARATION TIME	50 minutes
EQUIPMENT	kitchen foil

INGREDIENTS

500 g (1 lb 2 oz) root vegetables like celeriac, parsnips or beetroot (beets), or a mixture of root veg
3 tbsp Christmas Tree Ash (page 71)
a handful of thyme sprigs
salt and fresh ground black pepper
a glug of olive oil
120 ml (4 fl oz/½ cup) water

METHOD

Preheat the oven to 200°C (400°F/gas 7).

Chop the vegetables into 1 cm (½ in) wide pieces and arrange them in a casserole dish (Dutch oven), then dress them with a good helping of Christmas tree ash, the thyme sprigs, salt, pepper, a generous glug of olive oil and the water.

Cover the baking dish with kitchen foil and bake for 45 minutes until the vegetables are soft inside and crispy around the edges. Serve warm.

Ash Honey Glaze

This ash glaze is a very versatile cooking ingredient. It can be brushed generously over meat, fish, vegetables or even pastries like cinnamon buns before baking for a sweet, earthy and smoky flavour.

MAKES	Enough to glaze 400 g (14 oz)
PREPARATION TIME	15 minutes to make, then 2 hours to set
INGREDIENTS	70 g (2½ oz) honey 2 tsp Christmas Tree 50 ml (1¾ fl oz/3 tbsp) Ash (page 71) water
METHOD	In a small saucepan, heat the honey, water and the Christmas tree ash until just boiled.

Leave the glaze to cool then put it in the refrigerator to thicken for a couple of hours before using.

Use the glaze on vegetables, meat or fish before and during baking. Use on baked goods, like cinnamon buns, immediately after removing them from the oven.

Christmas Tree Hot-Smoked Fish

Hot smoking in an oven does have a few steps involved, but it's actually very straight forward. Cod, hake and haddock all smoke well, but you can also try smoking seafood like muscles or prawns. Serve with steamed spring greens like choy sum, a little lemon juice and some olive oil.

MAKES Enough for 2 people as a main

PREPARATION TIME 2 hours or overnight soaking,
then 2.5 hours prep and smoking time

EQUIPMENT a metal sieve (fine mesh strainer) or perforated steamer lid, a cooking pot that the sieve/steamer fits into well and a lid that sits tightly over the sieve/steamer

INGREDIENTS

500 ml (17 fl oz/2 cups) water
2 heaped tbsp caster (superfine) sugar
50 g (2 oz/½ cup) sea salt
peel and juice of 1 lemon
peel and juice of 1 orange
1 tsp crushed juniper berries
400 g (14 oz) fish or tofu
plenty of Christmas tree branches

METHOD Make a brine of water, sugar, salt, lemon and orange juice and peel, and juniper berries. Add the fish or tofu to the brine and leave in an airtight container in the refrigerator for at least 2 hours (or overnight).

Pack the bottom of the cooking pot with tree branches and heat them on the hob until most have started to blacken. Once blackened, take them out of the pot and double line the pot with kitchen foil. Place the blackened tree branches on the foil and seal the pot with the lid so that no aromas escape.

Place the marinated fish or tofu on top of the sieve/steamer and place inside the pot and seal. Turn the heat to high so that the tree branches begin to smoke again. Once the smoke is going strong, turn the heat down to very low and leave the smoke to infuse for 2 hours.

Scent Of The Pine

by Julia Georgallis

A walk through the woods.

Meandering past a long line of trees on a cold winter's morning, wrapped in hat and scarf, dog in tow, twigs and branches dusted in snow. Sauntering through the forest in the summer, sunlight dancing its way through the trees on the walk back from a beach, slightly sunburnt and grateful for the leafy shade. Hiking through jungle, pushing past branches that claw their way downwards and sideways and upwards and any which way, searching for soil in the undergrowth...

These are some of our memories of the pleasures of being sur-rounded by trees: in woods, forests or jungles, in parks, bushes, thickets or wilderness. Walking amongst trees is possibly one of the most naturally luxurious things we can do, often undertaken only when we have enough time on our hands. Forests are to be made time for, because they were built by time itself. Time to a tree is a totally different entity from time to man. The average tree (though, in truth, there is no such thing, just as there is no such thing as an average human) lives to at least 400 years old. Indeed, a tree is not really considered an adult until it is at least 150 years old.[1] No wonder, then, that they can so easily demand that we slow down.

Is it because of their slowness that trees give us such a sense of calm, or is it perhaps something else? Their size, for example, pacifies us. The rustle of leaves and the darkness of the forest floor often makes us fall silent. On a physical level, the forest provides us with our most basic needs: food, shelter, materials. On a metaphysical level, the forest humbles us, gives us perspec-tive and sparks creativity, making appearances in every creative pursuit of man – poems, literature, folklore, religion and belief systems, art, music and dance – as a place of magic and deep contemplation, and an enabler of ritual. But the most powerful magic that trees (and indeed all plants and flowers) hold over humans is in their scent. The aromas of trees and plants can be invigorating, inspirational, calming, healing and much more. As aromatherapist Julia Lawless writes, 'From the earliest times, herbs have been used as magic amulets to protect from evil spir-its or to bring good fortune, incense has traditionally been burnt at religious or ritual occasions to help transport the mind to an-other dimension, perfumes have been created to enrapture pro-spective lovers with their fragrances and the power of essential oils has long been associated with alchemy and the quest for an "elixir of life"...[2]'.

Aromatherapy, the use of scent for healing, has been practiced for centuries. There is a magic in smell, a belief that it brings us power, something bigger than ourselves, as it exists in an intangible realm. We sense smell but cannot see it, in the same way that we sense but cannot see our souls, feelings and thoughts. Indeed, the use of fragrance was deemed so powerful around the birth of Christianity that it was banned: '...in the Church's eyes, the human body and its natural instincts were something to be regarded with distrust and repulsion and, since perfume and incense stimulated the senses and could be used to heighten sensual pleasure, they were rejected...' [3]

Over the course of history, different smells had a plethora of different applications: frankincense for ritual, cedar for sensuality, lavender for relaxation. But it is the scent of the pine that has stood the test of time, having been used in everything from sun rituals to air fresheners, filling thousands of cars as it dangles on dashboards in the shape of a Christmas tree. 'Scent of the pine, you know how I feel,'[4] sings Nina Simone. Evergreen smells – pine, spruce, fir and juniper – are uplifting and rejuvenating. This is because the chemical compounds they contain, in particular those found in *pinus sylvestris*, stimulates 'the adrenal cortex and [are] an excellent pulmonary antiseptic'[5] – they make us clear-brained and clear-lunged. Pine smell also 'has a stimulating effect on the circulation,'[6] pumping blood through our body and letting us feel more energised. It is the archetypal 'clean' smell associated with purification and hygiene. And, as if the human nose knew it, there is scientific evidence to suggest that this is indeed true. Coniferous forests disinfect the air around them, and spruce and pine needles contain in-built antibiotic.[7]

Science aside, it is hard to dislike the smell of pine and evergreens in general. For many, this penetrating fragrance evokes vast, untouched wilderness, a limitless feeling that allows our minds to soar. Experience also impacts on our relationship with the scent of the pine. Our complicated sense of smell, linked to our central nervous system, often triggers memories. When we smell something, 'there is a direct contact between the molecules of the scent and our own receptors – it is an intimate or essential type of encounter'[8]. Smell, therefore, is subjective and personal, often transporting us to a thousand different places inside ourselves, sparking memories buried deep between nose and brain. In this case, to a time when we experienced the pine's invigorating smell: a pleasant walk high up in the fresh mountain air or finding solace in pine forests from the hot sun on a Mediterranean island.

A most recent conifer-scented experience of mine involved visiting a Christmas tree farm in High Easter, Essex, in December – down an empty road, deer in the neighbouring field watching curiously, winter sun low. And when the car door opened, the

smell that hit me was intense: the smell of tree upon tree upon tree, intertwined with the smell of cold air, mud and mid-winter. On visiting the same farm a few months later, however, I found the scent substantially different as the ends of each tree were now laced with new, bright green branches. The smell was sweeter, a bit like freshly cut grass. We are aware of how the smell of flowers can change – some smell strongest at night or in the early morning, blossom is most pungent in the spring – but this was my first experience of really appreciating how the smell of something that is considered as passive as a tree also changes. Trees, in fact, are not passive at all. It has become a widely accepted fact that they have something resembling a brain. They feel. They think. They see. They can even count![9] And, like us, they communicate. One of the ways they do it is through smell. To encourage pollinators, trees, like flowers, release scents to coax bees and birds to them. Should a predator land on a branch and launch an attack, trees also have the capacity to release a scent to repel the unwelcome guest and alert other trees to the incursion.[10] Humans, in many senses, are predators to a tree. Is it, then, possible that the scent of the forest is not a benign odour to benefit humans, but actually a distress signal, to alert the forest to our presence? The reason, perhaps, is obvious. Trees provide food, water and homes for creatures great and small, influence our weather, shepherd our land, keep our atmosphere at an optimum level for us to breathe. And yet, globally, forests are deteriorating. We make use of every part of the tree – from root to shoot, bark to bough. We fell them for farmland, clear forests to build our homes. We even distil their smell, greedily, for our own control, using it to please, dominate and attract. Throughout history, religion has offered scents to please gods and pacify followers; legend has it that Cleopatra would cover her sail boats in fragrance so that it would catch on the wind and make its way to the noses of her admirers in far-away lands.[11] As the notorious fictional murderer, Grenouille, believes in Patrick Süskind's *Perfume*, 'he who ruled scent ruled the hearts of man...'[12]

The scent that a tree gives, however, may not be intended for our exclusive benefit and should not be domesticated. It is produced for the trees' own survival and the survival of their habitat. Trees give us a great many things, and we seem to give very little back. Is it any wonder that they see us as an invading species? So, the next time you are walking through the park on a Sunday, or find yourself lost in the woods and catch the fragrance of the trees, perhaps adjust your nose and understand that a peaceful forest might actually be, in fact, odourless...

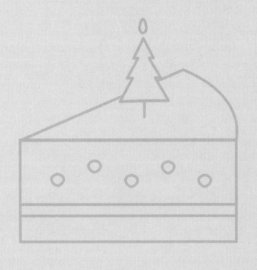

Sweet Treats

Christmas Tree
& Ginger Ice Cream

This is hands down my favourite recipe from the supper club, and I have shared it generously over the years with anyone who will listen. I like to use blue spruce, as I think it is the champion of conifers (it tastes a little like vanilla), but, as with all these recipes, you can interchange the type of Christmas tree you use depending on what you have access to.

MAKES 950 g (2 lb 2 oz) of ice cream

PREPARATION TIME 2 hours with an ice-cream maker, 4 hours without one

INGREDIENTS

300 g (10½ oz) blue spruce needles or 400 g (14 oz) any other type of Christmas tree needles
510 ml (17 fl oz/2 cups) double (heavy) cream
170 ml (6 fl oz/¾ cup) whole (full-fat) milk (ideally Jersey milk)
170 g (6 oz/¾ cup) caster (superfine) sugar
8 egg yolks
5 pieces stem ginger, chopped

METHOD

Prepare the needles (page 15).

In a heavy-bottomed saucepan whisk the cream, milk, sugar and egg yolks until well combined.

Add the needles to the cream mixture and heat gently, stirring continuously so that the mixture doesn't catch on the bottom or sides of the pan.

After 15 minutes, turn the heat up to medium. When bubbles begin to appear around the edge of the pan, the custard is ready and can be removed from the heat.

Sieve the mixture two or three times through a fine sieve (fine mesh strainer) so that none of the needles end up in the final ice cream mixture.

If using an ice-cream maker, add the sieved mixture to the churning pot and begin the churning process. Before it freezes, add the chopped stem ginger and continue churning until it is frozen. Transfer the frozen ice cream to the freezer.

If you don't own an ice-cream maker, transfer the mixture to a tub or dish and leave to cool completely. Once cooled, transfer to the freezer. Stir the mixture every hour and when it is beginning to freeze (about 2 hours) but not completely solid, add the chopped stem ginger and mix well. Continue stirring each hour until the ice cream is completely frozen. This will take about 4 hours.

Once it is frozen, keep it in the freezer until ready to serve.

See recipe photo overleaf.

Salted Pine Nut Brittle

This brittle is a luxurious festive gift to give but also works really well sprinkled on top of ice cream or baked into desserts. The key ingredient is smoked sea salt, which tastes delicious with the sweetness of the caramel.

MAKES	Fills a 30-cm (12-in) baking tray (sheet pan)
PREPARATION TIME	20 minutes
EQUIPMENT	a silicone spatula

INGREDIENTS

300 g (10½ oz/ 1⅓ cups) caster (superfine) sugar
200 g (7 oz/1⅓ cups) pine nuts, crushed

1 heaped tbsp unsalted butter, melted
3 big pinches of sea salt flakes, preferably smoked

METHOD

Line a shallow baking tray (sheet pan) with baking parchment.

Heat the sugar in a saucepan, first on a high heat and then, once it has started to melt, on a medium-low heat. Stir continuously for about 10 minutes until it becomes a dark, clear, caramel-colour and starts to smell like caramel. If you are using a sugar thermometer, you are aiming for 150°C (300°F).

Add the crushed pine nuts and butter to the caramel mixture and cook for a couple of minutes more. At the last minute, add the salt and give it a stir.

Pour the mixture into the lined baking tray, spreading it evenly with a silicone spatula so that it is ½ cm thick. Leave to set for an hour or so in the refrigerator.

Once hard and completely set, break the brittle into pieces and store in an airtight container. If it doesn't break easily, you can put it in the freezer for 10 minutes.

See recipe photo on previous page.

Coconut & Bamboo Ice Cream

Bamboo is often used in curries along with coconut milk. Here, I have used this winning combination for a sweet, rather than savoury, dish. Bamboo shoots don't have a huge amount of flavour, but they are soft, delicious and chewy, and hold other flavours well. It is best to use brined or pre-prepared bamboo shoots for this recipe – they are easy to find at Asian supermarkets and much easier to cook with than fresh shoots.

MAKES 1 kg (2 lb 4 oz) of ice cream

PREPARATION TIME 2 hours with an ice-cream maker, 4 hours without one

INGREDIENTS
1 x 400 ml (14 fl oz) tin of coconut milk
200 ml (7 fl oz/¾ cup) coconut cream
200 ml (7 fl oz/¾ cup) double (heavy) cream
4 egg yolks, whisked
300 g (10½ oz) caster (superfine) sugar
2 tsp vanilla bean paste
250 g (9 oz) bamboo in brine, chopped

METHOD Combine all the ingredients in a saucepan, apart from the bamboo, and stirring continuously over a medium heat.

When little bubbles start to form at the sides of the pan, turn the heat up and bring to the boil for a few seconds.

If you are using an ice-cream maker, transfer the mixture to the churning drum. Begin the churning process, adding the chopped bamboo before it freezes. Churn for 2 hours. Place in the freezer.

If you don't own an ice-cream maker, transfer the mixture to a tub or dish and leave to cool completely. Once cooled, transfer to the freezer. Stir the mixture every hour and, when it is beginning to freeze (about 2 hours in), add the chopped bamboo and mix well. Continue stirring each hour until the ice cream is completely frozen. This will take about 4 hours.

Once it is frozen, keep it in the freezer until ready to serve.

Tip: White pine tea can be
bought in specialist tea shops
or online, but if it is difficult to
find, use olive leaf tea instead.

Olive Oil, Lemon & White Pine Sorbet

The warm flavours of olive oil pair well with gentle white pine and a little bit of lemon. This sorbet works really well either as a palette cleanser between meals or for dessert. Use aquafaba instead of eggs to create a vegan sorbet alternative.

MAKES 900 g (2 lb) of sorbet

PREPARATION TIME 2 hours with an ice-cream maker,
4 hours without one (make the tea the day before!)

INGREDIENTS
200 g (7 oz/scant 1 cup) caster (superfine)sugar
500 ml (17 fl oz/2 cups) white pine, olive leaf tea or brewed Christmas Tree Tea (page 117), brewed the day before

200 ml (7 fl oz/scant 1 cup) olive oil
juice and zest of 1 lemon
4 egg whites or 8 tbsp of aquafaba, whisked into soft peaks

METHOD In a small saucepan, heat the sugar and tea together until just boiled.

If you are using an ice-cream maker, leave to churn for 30 minutes, then add the whisked egg whites or aquafaba and churn for another hour and 15 minutes.

If you are not using an ice-cream maker, whisk for 10 more minutes then add the whisked egg whites or aquafaba. Whisk for another 15 minutes, leave the mixture to cool, then pop it in the freezer. Whisk for 5 minutes every hour for 4 hours.

Keep in the freezer until ready to serve.

Pine Nut & Chocolate Brownie

This recipe is inspired by the traditional Italian dessert *torta di pinoli e cioccolato*. The oils in the pine nuts make this brownie very moist and fudgey, and the creamy, nutty flavour works well with chocolate.

MAKES 8 brownies

PREPARATION TIME 1 hour

INGREDIENTS

200 g (7 oz/1⅓ cups) pine nuts
150 g (5 oz) dark chocolate
150 g (5 oz) milk chocolate
170 g (6 oz) unsalted butter, plus extra for greasing

5 large organic free-range eggs
300 g (10½ oz/ 1⅓ cups) caster (superfine) sugar
130 g (4 oz/1 cup) plain (all-purpose) flour
2 pinches of sea salt

METHOD

Preheat the oven to 180°C (350°F/gas 6).

Crush 150 g (5 oz) of the pine nuts in a pestle and mortar. Melt the chocolate, butter and the crushed pine nuts over a bain-marie.

While the chocolate is melting, whisk the eggs and sugar together until the sugar has dissolved.

Pour the egg and sugar mix into the melted chocolate mixture and beat so that you have a glossy texture.

Stir the flour with a couple of pinches of sea salt and fold into the chocolate mixture, adding a little bit at a time until it is all combined.

Line a 20-cm (8-in) baking tin with baking parchment and grease with butter. Pour in the brownie mixture, sprinkling the remaining 50 g (2 oz) of pine nuts over the top.

Bake for 20 minutes. You will know that it's ready when cracks have formed around the edge of the brownie. The middle should be quite gooey. Either serve hot if you want a gooey consistency or set in the refrigerator overnight.

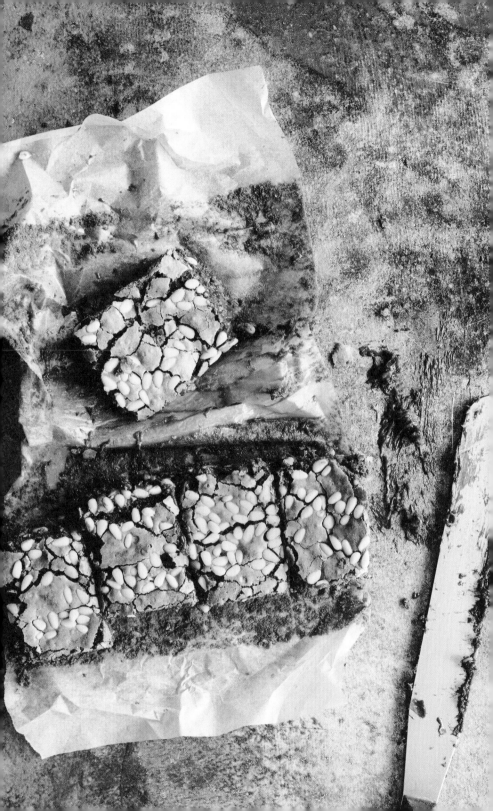

Plum & Juniper Crumble

Both plums and juniper are very versatile ingredients and come together to make an excellent, easy-going couple. Both hold the same cultural significance as traditional Christmas trees for being hardy, plucky and symbols of resilience. Serve hot with ice cream or custard.

MAKES Enough for 10 people

PREPARATION TIME 45 minutes

INGREDIENTS

8 tsp juniper berries
1 punnet plums, destoned and chopped
juice of 1 lemon
200 g (7 oz/scant 1 cup) caster (superfine) sugar
70 g (2½ oz/⅔ cup) ground almonds (almond meal)

70g (2½ oz/generous ½ cup) walnuts, chopped
100 g (3½ oz/generous ¾ cup) plain (all-purpose) flour
150 g (5 oz) unsalted butter, plus extra for greasing
1 tsp ground nutmeg
1 tsp ground cinnamon

METHOD

Preheat the oven to 180°C (350°F/gas 6).

Crush up juniper berries in a pestle and mortar and put them in a mixing bowl. Add the chopped plums, lemon juice and 100 g (3½ oz) of the sugar to the bowl. Mix and leave to stand while you make the crumble topping.

For the topping, mix the ground almonds, chopped walnuts, flour, butter, ground nutmeg, ground cinnamon and the rest of the sugar in a bowl with your fingertips until the mixture resembles breadcrumbs.

Grease a deep 30-cm (12-in) baking tin or glass oven dish then arrange the plum mixture in the bottom of the dish, topped with the crumble.

Bake in the oven for 35 minutes until slightly browned on top.

Drinks

Christmas Tree Cordial

Christmas tree cordial, especially if you are using spruce, tastes a bit like grapefruit juice and rather than turning green, as you might expect, will turn a colour ranging from bright orange to pastel pink. You can use either fir or spruce, or a mixture of both – I don't recommend making it with pine as the flavour is a bit too weak and gets overpowered by the sugar and lemons. The flavour of this cordial is quite expansive and zingy.

MAKES 2 litres (70 fl oz/8 cups) of cordial

PREPARATION TIME 2 hours

EQUIPMENT a 2-litre (70-fl-oz/8-cup) glass bottle with a lid

INGREDIENTS
juice of 10 lemons, zest of 4
2 litres (70 fl oz/8 cups) water
700 g (1 lb 9 oz/ 3 cups) caster (superfine) sugar
400 g (14 oz) spruce and/or fir needles (you can also use some of the branches to add flavour)

METHOD Sterilise the glass bottle (page 15).

Bring the lemon juice and zest, water, sugar and needles to the boil over a medium-high heat. Turn the heat down to low and simmer for 2 hours.

Take the pan off the heat and strain through a fine sieve (fine mesh strainer) to remove the needles. Do this a few times to ensure that there are no needles left in the mixture. Pour the mixture, using a funnel, into the sterilised bottle.

Leave to cool and refrigerate. This keeps for a couple of weeks in the refrigerator.

Opposite are some great festive cocktails you can try, using this cordial. Give it a go!

Christmas Tree Cordial-based Cocktails

MAKES Enough for 2 cocktails

PREPARATION TIME 15 minutes each

Christmas Tree Sour

INGREDIENTS 50 ml (1¾ oz/3 tbsp) Christmas Tree Cordial (see opposite)
100 ml (3½ fl oz/scant ⅓ cup) sparkling water
100 ml (3½ fl oz/scant ⅓ cup) bourbon or a non-alcoholic spirit
like Seedlip or Smreka (page 113)
3 drops of Angostura bitters
a large ice cube
juice of 2 limes

Christmas Tree Mimosa

INGREDIENTS 70 ml (2½ fl oz/5 tbsp) Christmas Tree Cordial (see opposite)
140 ml (5 fl oz/scant ⅔ cup) prosecco
a large ice cube
a slice of lemon

METHOD To make either cocktail, combine all the ingredients, including the ice, preferably in a cocktail shaker and shake rapidly for a minute. If you don't have a cocktail shaker, use a jar with a lid instead.

Pour into a cold glass and serve.

Christmas Tree Booze Infusions

A note about drinking Christmas trees: Christmas trees and evergreens could now be considered a bar staple, with mixologists using their woody flavours in cocktails. But this is nothing new; many mountain communities have been using flavours such as spruce, fir and juniper in distilled spirits for generations – take Alpine génépy or Scandinavian snaps. Indeed, juniper is the key component of gin.

Again, these recipes are a good way of using up any dry Christmas trees and, as with the cordial, you can also use the bark as well as the needles. Making these with either pine, fir or spruce in the days after Christmas means you'll have festively flavoured booze to last you well into the New Year. I have suggested three different infusion options. Each of these recipes can be made interchangeably with spruce, fir or pine and you can use either gin or vodka as a base alcohol.

MAKES	1 litre (34 fl oz/4 cups) of alcohol

EQUIPMENT	2 x 1-litre (34-fl-oz/4-cup) glass jar, or bottle with a wide neck, with a lid, a Kilner or Mason jar is ideal

BASE INGREDIENTS	1 litre (34 fl oz/4 cups) good quality vodka or gin	2 large handfuls of spruce, fir or pine (branches included!)

Spicy Infusion (best made with fir)

INFUSION TIME	4 days	
INGREDIENTS	1 tsp crushed cardamom pods	3 cinnamon sticks 3 star anise

Botanical Infusion (best made with spruce)

INFUSION TIME	1 week	
INGREDIENTS	a small handful of rosemary ½ tsp of crushed juniper berries	a small handful of sage leaves

Uplifting Infusion (best made with pine)

INFUSION TIME	1 week	
INGREDIENTS	peel of ½ lemon 2.5 cm (1 in) piece of ginger, finely chopped	peel of ½ orange

METHOD	Sterilise the glass jars or bottles and wash the Christmas tree branches (page 15). As you are not cutting the needles from the branches, it is imperative that you do this thoroughly as bits of dirt might still be left on the bark.

Add your washed tree branch, vodka or gin and chosen infusions to the sterilised jar.

Seal the jar, ensuring it is airtight and leave it somewhere dark for up to a week (see infusion times above). Your booze will turn anything from yellow to red to brown as it infuses. Strain the infused booze through a fine sieve (fine mesh strainer) and discard everything else.

Pour into a fresh sterilised bottle. Once infused, it keeps for a long time!

Infusion-based Cocktails

MAKES   Enough for 2 cocktails

PREPARATION TIME   15 minutes each

Cranberry Martini with Spicy Infusion

INGREDIENTS

70 ml (2 fl oz/5 tbsp)
Spicy Infusion
(page 105)
1 tbsp orange liqueur

30 ml (1 fl oz/1½ tbsp)
dry vermouth
100 ml (3½ fl oz/scant
½ cup) cranberry juice

Lemon Fizz with Botanical Infusion

INGREDIENTS

120 ml (24 fl oz/½ cup)
Botanical Infusion
(page 105)
60 ml (2 fl oz/¼ cup)
agave syrup or
Christmas Tree Cordial
(page 102)

juice of 3 lemons
4 egg whites, beaten
a glug of soda water

Cucumber Cooler with Uplifting Infusion

INGREDIENTS

130 ml (4 fl oz/½ cup)
Uplifting Infusion
(page 105)
6 large, peeled
cucumber slices

150 g (5 oz/1 cup) ice
a glug of tonic water

METHOD   To make each cocktail, combine all the ingredients (including the ice when making the cucumber cooler) preferably in a cocktail shaker and shake rapidly for a minute. If you don't have a cocktail shaker, use a jar with a lid instead.

Pour into a cold glass and serve.

These are some of my favourite cocktails to make, using the booze infusions from the previous page.

Boozey Christmas Tree Shots

If you want to be reminded of being 18 again, Christmas tree jelly shots are the way to do it. Use any of the booze infusions (page 105) to make these.

MAKES 5 servings of jelly

INFUSION TIME 15 minutes to make, at least 1 hour setting time

EQUIPMENT moulds – you can use ice cube trays, proper jelly moulds or a glass container. If you are going to serve these as desserts, you could also set these in shot glasses.

INGREDIENTS 250 ml (8½ fl oz/1 cup) Christmas Tree Booze Infusion of your choice (page 105)

½ sachet of vegetarian setting gel powder (1 tsp) Christmas tree sprigs, washed thoroughly

METHOD In a saucepan, heat the alcohol until just boiled.

Measure out the teaspoon of vegetarian setting gel powder into a mixing bowl. Once the alcohol has boiled, take the saucepan off the heat and pour the hot booze infusion over the setting gel powder, whisking well so that there is absolutely no trace of the powder left.

Add a sprig of tree to the moulds that you are using. Pour the booze infusion jelly mixture into the mould and let it set for 1 hour.

Keeps in the refrigerator for up to 2 weeks.

Smreka

This is a Bosnian fermented drink made from juniper berries, which is both festive and refreshing, so is also good served on summer days. Juniper berries house a lot of yeast on their skins – this is the reason why they ferment so well. This can be extremely bitter – juniper has lots of medicinal properties and can taste a little bit like crushed-up paracetamol tablets if you let the fermentation go too far. You can use this Smreka as a gin or vodka substitute for non-alcoholic versions of the cocktails in the previous recipes (pages 103–109).

MAKES 2 litres (70 fl oz/8 cups) of Smreka

PREPARATION TIME 15 minutes + up to 10 days fermentation time

EQUIPMENT 2-litre (70-fl-oz/8-cup) glass Kilner or Mason jar/jar with a lid + some sterilised bottles for the finished Smreka mixture

INGREDIENTS
1 unwaxed lemon, washed and sliced into quarters
75 g (2½ oz/scant 1 cup) juniper berries
2 litres (70 fl oz/8 cups) water
2 tsp caster (superfine) sugar or honey

METHOD Sterilise the glass jars and bottles (page 15). Add the lemon and the juniper berries to the sterilised jar, then fill with water and add the sugar or honey.

Seal the jar and leave in a sunny place for 1–2 weeks until all the juniper berries have sunk to the bottom of the jar, giving the jar a shake every now and again to encourage the juniper berries to sink.

The amount of time that you choose to ferment your juniper berries and the environment they are fermented in will make a difference to the flavour. For example, a two-week ferment in a humid kitchen leads to a bitter taste; one week in a cooler place will lead to a lighter flavour.

When the mixture has turned a pale yellow, strain out the berries and lemons. Use a funnel to pour the Smreka into a fresh sterilised bottle and keep in the refrigerator until ready to drink. Keeps for about a week in the refrigerator.

Smreka-based Cocktails

MAKES	Enough for 2 cocktails
PREPARATION TIME	15 minutes each

Simply on its own

Simply, on its own with ice, a slice of lemon and a few dried juniper berries to garnish.

Elderflower, Smreka & Champagne

INGREDIENTS

70 ml (2½ fl oz/5 tbsp) Champagne
30 ml (1 fl oz/2 tbsp) elderflower cordial

50 ml (1¾ fl oz/3 tbsp) Smreka (page 113)
a few ice cubes

Non-alcoholic Smreka Mule

INGREDIENTS

a small bunch of chopped mint leaves
30 ml (1 fl oz/2 tbsp) lemon juice
30 ml (1 fl oz/2 tbsp) honey
50 ml (1¾ fl oz/3 tbsp) Smreka

50 ml (1¾ fl oz/3 tbsp) ginger beer (you can always opt for alcoholic ginger beer!)
a few ice cubes

METHOD

To make each cocktail, combine all the ingredients, including the ice, preferably in a cocktail shaker and shake rapidly for a minute. If you don't have a cocktail shaker, use a jar with a lid instead.

Pour into a cold glass and serve.

The bitter, refreshing taste of Smreka lends itself to cocktail making and is a great alcohol substitute because of its similarities to gin.

Christmas Tree Tea

Christmas Tree Tea is one of the first things that comes to mind when we think about what we can do with leftover Christmas tree branches. Boiling the needles was one of the first ports of call for the How to Eat Your Christmas Tree supper club research. Apparently, pine, fir and spruce contain a lot of vitamin C, but simply brewing them on their own with hot water doesn't produce the most interesting of flavours – pine in particular is quite weak, although it does have a delicate, warming taste. If you don't have pine, fir or spruce then you can also buy Scots pine, white pine or olive leaf tea, which are already dried and ready for brewing.

MAKES	A pot full of tea (about 650 ml/22 fl oz/2¾ cups)
PREPARATION TIME	6 minutes
INGREDIENTS	a handful of pine, fir or spruce needles juice of a lemon a kettle of water 30 ml (1 fl oz/2 tbsp) honey
METHOD	Prepare the needles (page 15). Take a handful of needles, boil some water and brew in a teapot for 6 minutes. Add a dash of lemon juice and 2 teaspoons of honey to each cup. Then pour over the brewed tree tea and serve.

Scandinavian Taste Buds

by Amanda Skaar

If you've ever imagined Scandinavians as outdoorsy types and nature lovers, then you're not far from the truth. A study by Professor Fereshteh Ahmadi at the University of Gävle highlights 'nature' as Sweden's main belief system[1] – in fact, it has replaced modern-day religion for many Swedes. In the same study, an investigation of nationwide responses from more than 2,400 cancer patients on how they are dealing with their disease revealed that 68 per cent of patients said they turned to nature, while only 14 per cent went to church; pointing at how Swedish society has become accustomed to seeking out nature during life crises.

Norway, which topped the happiness index in 2017[2] and 2019, also has a very special relationship with the great outdoors. Recent research by the Norwegian newspaper *Dagsavisen*[3] showed that nine out of 10 Norwegians are interested in outdoor activities and eight out of 10 take advantage of their natural surroundings by walking, running, skiing or enjoying other types of al fresco recreational activities.

Harvest, a Norwegian magazine dedicated to investigating human connections with nature, frequently highlights such experiences, and interviews individuals around the country who have found peace by being outside. Norwegian researcher, Åse Dragland, has shown that contact with green areas and animals is a fundamental necessity for Norwegian citizens, not only to maintain health but also to feel a sense of belonging and meaning in life. She also discovered that children who experienced stressful incidents were better prepared to tackle them if they were living in more rural or greener environments. Similarly, children who experienced bullying, family break-ups or moving from one place to another, found comfort and stability when they had more access to the outdoors.

One of the main reasons Scandinavia has become an increasingly interesting tourism destination is not just because of its natural wonders, which have been around for millennia, but also because of the recent innovations that celebrate nature through food, architecture and holistic experiences. Snøhetta, a Norwegian architecture firm, was recently listed as one of Fast Company's Top Innovators in 2019, and is often celebrated for its ability to connect humans to the environment: hospital retreat cabins integrated into forest landscapes, hotel rooms soaring in treetops and, most recently, an underwater restaurant, are just a few of the innovations the company has made possible by leveraging its vision of the natural world. Scandinavian chefs continue to be recognised for their ability to work with food sourced locally in a typically dry, cold and not particularly varied environment. René Redzepi and Mads Refslund have been known, for example, to cook with ingredients such as spruce, moss and other native plants by using them in salads, creating pickled snacks, or infused into cocktails and syrups. This desire to harness nature for our own well-being takes place on a much smaller scale in an average Scandinavian's day-to-day life, too.

My grandmother, Maj-Britt, has always had a profound connection to the natural world around her – as a young woman, she ran her own shop, selling her own handmade products crafted from things like rye straw, as well as locally produced, artisan textiles and homewares, and my grandfather's paintings of the Swedish landscapes in Dalsland where they lived.

At 50, my grandmother started using the forest to innovate in her kitchen. She had already been inspired by several trips to the French Riviera in the 1950s, where she had cooked for grandpa and his painter entourage who would spend summers in Salernes. Inspired by French cuisine, which often celebrates local, artisanal ingredients, Maj-Britt applied this philosophy to the local dishes of Dalsland and soon became a famous host of dinner parties. Having developed recipes around her foraging trips and her extensive knowledge of mushroom varieties, she could easily whip up dishes from ingredients that were growing close at hand: wild strawberries, rhubarb and elderflower were her dessert staples, while savoury dishes always contained a sprinkling of cepes and chanterelles. There would always be bunches of spruce left over from foraging trips in her mushroom basket and, if she was feeling particularly apathetic about searching for food that day, she would start chewing on spruce buds – lime green, soft, citrusy and captivating, and she has continued to make a habit of it. 'Every spring, when I'm out on my little walks in the forest behind the house, I tend to pluck the freshly green spruces and chew on them, just because they taste so good. I didn't start eating spruces until my 50s when I moved out here to Flatebyn, and no one really told me about them. I just knew, like with certain mushrooms, that these things won't poison you, so you might as well try. I've always been curious about the so-called superfoods you can find

'Every spring, when I'm out on walks in the forest, I tend to pluck the freshly green spruces and chew on them... Maybe it was these green sprouts that gave my body the little extra kick it needed to make it to 90 this year?'

in your own garden – maybe it was these green sprouts that gave my body the little extra kick it needed to make it to 90 this year?'

It's not just the Swedish side of my family that developed a liking for spruce. Olav, my Norwegian cousin, has also harnessed their grassy, fresh flavours in his cooking. After inheriting his family's farm, Langsrud, Olav set in motion a renewed focus on self-sufficiency by increasing the number of hens and sheep at the farm, replanting crops, and venturing out in his own forest to find new sources of nutrition. As Olav continued the tradition of harvesting his own Christmas trees, one spring he started testing out new uses for his evergreens and was drawn to the beautiful new spruce buds – just as my grandmother had been in a different part of Scandinavia. After reading extensively about the benefits of spruce, Olav began testing recipes. He soon discovered that his daughter, Alma, was a big fan of his spruce syrup, especially when paired with her morning pancakes or on Norwegian waffles. 'My wife and I were so happy to see how she devoured whole spoonfuls of the spruce syrup – apparently it's a great way to combat colds, and it seems to have worked so far!' Spruce, in both of these instances, was something inherently attractive to the members of my family, separated by two generations and, I am positive, to many other Scandis over the years. Before Christianity became the dominant religion, Scandinavians were indeed tree-worshippers of the biggest kind. We worshipped the many gods who we could find represented in nature. Spruce, in particular, was a well-respected plant, considered sacred and used in many old Norse and Sami rituals. The two stories from my own family make me wonder whether this innate understanding of the delicious things we can find on the forest floor, the tasty moss growing on logs, the berries we find high up on branches and the bright-green buds that blossom for us in the spring, is part of some deep-rooted knowledge. Perhaps we have a muscle-memory of these rituals, passed down to us somewhere, through a strand of shared DNA by ancestors who were also charmed by the beauty of these resilient trees and this seemingly barren but generous land.

Where Can I Buy An Edible Christmas Tree?

Austria
weihnachtsbaum.at

Belgium
uap.be

Canada
canadianchristmastrees.ca

Czech Republic
vanocnistromek.cz

Denmark
christmastree.de

Europe General Information
The Christmas Tree Growers
Council of Europe
ctgce.com

France
afsnn.fr

Germany
bvwe.de

Great Britain
British Christmas Tree
Growers Association
bctga.co.uk

Ireland
christmastreesireland.com

Norway
norskjuletre.no

Poland
orfo.pl

Portugal
You can rent pine trees that
are culled by the country's fire
service to prevent forest fires.
Once Christmas is over, the
fire service will collect your
tree and turn it into mulch for
agricultural projects.
https://www.facebook.com/
pinheirobombeiro.pt

Sweden
In Stockholm, trees are
recycled to create biochar
which is then used for
replanting projects in the city
to stabilise carbon emissions.

Switzerland
suisse-christbaum.ch

USA
National Christmas Tree
Association
realchristmastrees.org

Notes

***If We Stopped Harvesting
Christmas Trees – Processing Statistics,
pp. 24–25**

There are 3 trillion trees in the world,[1] 170
billion of these are at risk from destruction. It
is estimated that 40 million trees are harvested
each year at Christmas time in the USA[2] and UK[3]
alone.[4] These Christmas trees are cut down, on
average, after 7–10 years of growth. However,
the average life of a tree is around 400 years and
one tree will store approximately 22 tonnes of
carbon dioxide (CO_2) in its lifetime[5] – 22 tonnes
multiplied by 40 million equals 880 million tonnes
of CO_2 that could be stored if just one year's
worth of Christmas tree harvest survives. Globally,
all flights produced 859 million tonnes of carbon
emissions in 2017 alone.[6] That is only 21 million
tonnes short of 880 million – in other words, our
Christmas trees have a potential CO_2 capture
equivalent of just over one year's worth of carbon
emissions from all flights around the world. There
are 38.2 million cars on the roads in the UK[7] and
a standard passenger vehicle emits 4.6 tonnes of
carbon emissions per year globally[8] – 4.6 tonnes
multiplied by 38.2 million cars, equals 175,720
million tonnes of CO_2 emissions from the UK's cars
each year. This means the 40 million Christmas
trees harvested in the USA and UK each year have
a CO_2 capture potential equivalent to 20 per cent
of the annual carbon emissions of all the UK's cars.

Acknowledgements

To Lauren, for agreeing to eat trees with me!

To all the curious people who have joined my supper club over the years to eat Christmas trees with me.

To Charlotte, who provided me with trees to eat.

To Richard Brendon London for lending me some of his beautiful glassware.

Thank you to everyone at Hardie Grant and to Sophie Yamamoto for freshening up the design of this new edition.

And to the trees, for being so tasty.

Collaborators & Contributors

Reading stuff over/telling me what they think: Isla Binnie, Nadia Demosthenous, Zoe Georgallis, Karolina Klermon Williams, Sim Pereira-Madder and Molly Feely

'Scent of the Pine', words by Julia Georgallis/Photography by Carmel King

'Scandinavian Taste Buds', words by Amanda Skaar. Amanda is half Norwegian, half Swedish and currently works for Google in Dublin. She has previously worked in policy and corporate responsibilty for the International Chamber of Commerce, Paris.

About The Author

Julia is an artisan baker and industrial designer. She graduated from the Royal College of Art in 2014 before working as a baker in London for a while. Her work looks at food as a design solution and as an educative, empowering tool.

Follow This Project
Search for #howtoeatyourchristmastree on Instagram.
More information can be found at juliageorgallis.co.uk

References

Introduction, pp. 8–12

1. The Intergovernmental Panel on Climate Change, 2018, *Global Warming of 1.5°C*, viewed 14 November 2018, www.ipcc.ch/sr15/

2. Watts, J. 2018, 'We have 12 years to limit climate change catastrophe, warns UN', *The Guardian*, viewed 8 October 2018, www.theguardian.com/environment/2018/oct/08/global-warming-must-not-exceed-15c-warns-landmark-un-report

3. BBC News, 2019, 'UK Parliament declares climate change emergency', viewed 1 May 2019, www.bbc.co.uk/newsvwww.bbc.com/news/uk-politics-48126677

4. Wohlleben, P. 2017, *The Hidden Life of Trees*, Harper Collins, p. 93

5. UK Government, 'Plant a Tree Campaign', 2018, viewed 23 January 2019, www.london.gov.uk/what-we-do/environment/parksgreen-spaces-and-biodiversity/plant-tree/

6. Watts, J. 2019, 'Amazon fires: what is happening and is there anything we can do?' *The Guardian*, viewed 23 August 2019 www.theguardian.com/environment/2019/aug/23/amazon-fires-what-is-happening-anything-we-can-do

7. BBC News, 2018, 'Is the Amazon facing new dangers?', viewed 24 November 2018, https://www.bbc.com/news/world-46030592

8. Bastin, J., Finegold, Y., Garcia, C., Mollicone, D., Rezende, M., Routh, D., Zohner, C. M., Crowther, T. W. 2019, 'The global tree restoration potential', *Science Journal*, Vol. 365, Issue 6448, pp. 76–79

9. Young, E. 2012, 'Gut instincts: The secrets of your second brain,' *New Scientist*, viewed 18 November 2018, www.newscientist.com/article/mg21628951-900-gut-instincts-thesecrets-of-your-second-brain/

10. Bonneau, A. M. 2019, 'Environmental Guilt Syndrome,' viewed 3 March 2019, www.zerowastechef.com/2019/02/14/how-to-cope-withenvironmental-guilt-syndrome-egs/

How do I find a good tree to eat?, p. 14
1. Wendle, J. 2017, 'Gravity-Defying Villagers Risk Their Lives for Christmas Trees', *National Geographic*, viewed 21 February 2017, www.nationalgeographic.com/news/2017/12/georgiamountains-christmas-tree-harvesting-fair-trees-danger/

Have yourself a veggie little Christmas, p. 18
1. Jack, I. 2016, 'Christmas the season of goodwill to all men and cruelty to animals,' *The Guardian*, viewed 21 February 2020, www.theguardian.com/commentisfree/2016/dec/17/christmasseason-goodwill-cruelty-animals-vegetarians
2. Guyoncourt, S. 2019, 'The end of Christmas turkey? Waitrose reports 40% rise in vegan festive food', inews, viewed 21 February 2020, www.inews.co.uk/inews-lifestyle/food-and-drink/christmasdinner-vegan-food-waitrose-1343981

Scent of the Pine, pp. 77–81
1. Wohlleben, P. 2017, *The Hidden Life of Trees*, Harper Collins, p. 155
2. Lawless, J. 1994, *Aromatherapy and the Mind*, Thorsons, Introduction xii
3. Lawless, J. 1994, *Aromatherapy and the Mind*, Thorsons, p. 15
4. Leslie Bricusse, Anthony Newley, 'Feelin' Good,' written for the musical 'The roar of the greasepaint, the smell of the crowd,' 1964
5. Lawless, J. 1994, *Aromatherapy and the Mind*, Thorsons, p. 198
6. Lawless, J. 1994, *Aromatherapy and the Mind*, Thorsons, p. 198
7. Wohlleben, P. 2017, *The Hidden Life of Trees*, Harper Collins, p. 156
8. Lawless, J. 1994, *Aromatherapy and the Mind*, Thorsons, p. 51
9. Wohlleben, P. 2017, *The Hidden Life of Trees*, Harper Collins, p. 148
10. Wohlleben, P. 2017, *The Hidden Life of Trees*, Harper Collins, p. 7
11. Lawless, J. 1994, *Aromatherapy and the Mind*, Thorsons, p. 66
12. Süskind, P. 2010, *Perfume: The Story of a Murderer*, Penguin, p. 155

Scandinavian Taste Buds, pp. 121–123
1. Sjodin, A. 2015, 'Ny forskning: Naturen som en religion för svenskar', viewed 4 March 2019, www.arbetarbladet.se/artikel/ny-forskning-naturen-somen-religion-for-svenskar
2. World Happiness Index 2017, viewed 1 March 2019, worldhappiness.report/ed/2017/
3. Sandberg, T. 2012, 'Nordmenn elsker friluftsliv', viewed 1 March 2019, www.dagsavisen.no/innenriks/nordmenn-elskerfriluftsliv-1.474353

If We Stopped Harvesting Christmas Trees – Processing Statistics, p. 129
1. The Trillion Tree Campaign, viewed 3 November 2018, www.trilliontreecampaign.org
2. The National Christmas Tree Association, viewed 3rd November 2018, https://realchristmastrees.org/
3. The British Christmas Tree Growers Association, viewed 15 March 2019, www.bctga.co.uk
4. Quick Tree Facts, viewed 24 November 2018, www.realchristmastrees.org/dnn/Education/Quick-Tree-Facts
5. Wohlleben, P. 2017, *The Hidden Life of Trees*, Harper Collins, p. 93
6. The Air Transport Action Group, viewed 15 March 2019, www.atag.org
7. RAC (UK), viewed 15 March 2019, www.racfoundation.org/data
8. The US Environmental Protection Agency, viewed 15 March 2019, www.epa.gov

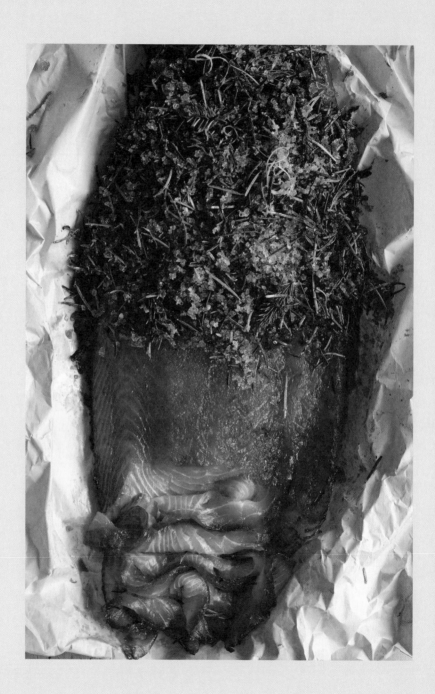

Index

First self-published in 2019 by Julia Georgallis
This hardback edition Published in 2020 by Hardie Grant Books,
an imprint of Hardie Grant Publishing

Hardie Grant Books (London)
5th & 6th Floors
52–54 Southwark Street
London SE1 1UN

Hardie Grant Books (Melbourne)
Building 1, 658 Church Street
Richmond, Victoria 3121

hardiegrantbooks.com

British Library Cataloguing-in-Publication Data. A catalogue
record for this book is available from the British Library.

How To Eat Your Christmas Tree
ISBN: 978-1-78488-371-3

10 9 8 7 6 5 4 3 2 1

Publishing Director: Kate Pollard
Commissioning Editor: Kajal Mistry
Editors: Eila Purvis and Alexandra Lidgerwood
Design and Art Direction: original book, Maru Studio, this
hardback edition, Sophie Yamamoto
Illustrations: Maru Studio (chapter openers), Jessica Hart (cover
and pages 24–25), © photoiget/Adobe Stock(page 30),
© derbisheva/Adobe Stock (pages 31, 32, 33), @ elyaka/Adobe
Stock (page 32)
Recipe Photographer: Lizzie Mayson
Food Stylist: Tamara Vos
Prop Stylist: Louie Waller
Copy Editor: Lisa Pendreigh
Proofreader: Sarah Herman
Indexer: Cathy Heath

Colour reproduction by p2d
Printed and bound in China by Leo Paper Products Ltd.